Chickenlicious

WeightWatchers®

Chickenlicious

BE INSPIRED BY OVER 40 DELICIOUS CHICKEN RECIPES

TAMSIN BURNETT-HALL

**SIMON &
SCHUSTER
ILLUSTRATED**

London · New York · Sydney · Toronto · New Delhi

A CBS COMPANY

The recipes

 ProPoints values: You'll find a **ProPoints** value beside every recipe in this book. This tells you how many **ProPoints** values per serving each recipe contains.

This symbol means that a recipe is suitable to eat on a Filling & Healthy day, so if you see it beside any of the recipes in this book then you can cook and eat it confident in the knowledge that you won't need to count anything at all.

Filling & Healthy Foods: We highlight all of our Filling & Healthy foods in green. These foods are at the heart of our plan so eat them where you can – they will help to fill you up faster and keep you fuller for longer.

 This means you can freeze this dish. There may be specific freezing instructions so just check the recipe to be sure.

If you see this symbol beside a recipe, it means that healthy oils (olive, safflower, sunflower, flaxseed or rapeseed) have been used – remember, if you're on a Filling & Healthy day and you have already used your 2 daily teaspoons, you'll need to count this out of your weekly allowance.

The small print

Eggs We use medium eggs, unless otherwise stated. Pregnant women, the elderly and children should avoid recipes with eggs which are not fully cooked or raw.

Fruit and Vegetables Our recipes use medium-sized fruit and veg unless otherwise stated.

Low fat spread When a recipe uses a low fat spread, we mean a spread with a fat content of no less than 38%.

Low fat soft cheese Where a recipe uses low fat soft cheese, we mean a soft cheese with a fat content of less than 5%.

Microwaves If we have used a microwave in any of our recipes, the timings will be for an 850 watt microwave oven.

Prep and cooking times These are approximate and meant to be guidelines. Prep time includes all the steps up to and following the main cooking time(s). Cooking times may vary according to your oven. Before serving chicken, always check that there is no pink meat and that the juices run clear by piercing with a sharp knife or skewer.

First published in Great Britain by
Simon & Schuster UK Ltd, 2014
A CBS Company

Copyright © 2014, Weight Watchers
International, Inc.

SIMON & SCHUSTER
ILLUSTRATED BOOKS
Simon & Schuster UK Ltd
222 Gray's Inn Road
London WC1X 8HB
www.simonandschuster.co.uk
Simon & Schuster Australia, Sydney
Simon & Schuster India, New Delhi

Weight Watchers, **ProPoints** and the
ProPoints icon are the registered trademarks
of Weight Watchers International Inc. and used
under license by Weight Watchers (UK) Ltd.
All rights reserved.

Weight Watchers Publications Team:
Imogen Prescott, Nicola Kirk, Nina McKerlie
Photography: William Shaw
Food preparation: Sue Ashworth
Prop styling: Liz Hippisley

For Simon & Schuster Illustrated
Director of Illustrated Publishing: Ami Stewart
Senior Commissioning Editor: Nicky Hill
Art Director: Corinna Farrow
Production Manager: Katherine Thornton
Design: Richard Proctor
Illustrations: Atlas Print Studio

Colour Reproduction by
Dot Gradations Ltd, UK
Printed and bound in Italy

A CIP catalogue record for this book
is available from the British Library

ISBN: 978-1-47113-708-2

Pictured on front cover, clockwise from top left: Delicious Chicken and Ratatouille Lasagne, page 106; Super-fast Curry, page 60; The Best Summer Salad, page 40; Smoky Roast Chicken and Vegetables, page 80; Must-try Asian-inspired Meatballs, page 96
Pictured on back cover from left to right: Easy Italian Chicken, Bean and Bacon Braise, page 76; Tarragon Chicken Burgers, page 98; Chicken in a Tomato and Chorizo Sauce, page 64
Pictured on front flap: One-pot Rosemary and Bacon Chicken Pasta, page 84
Pictured on back flap: Chicken Chilli Blanco, page 94

CONTENTS

INTRODUCTION

Where would we be without chicken?

It's easy to cook, almost endlessly versatile, tender and with a mild flavour that is a perfect base for adding in other ingredients and flavours. Ideal for both everyday family meals and also for special occasions, chicken is always a popular choice.

Chicken just works

Chicken works in almost any style of cooking: stir-frying, roasting, casseroling, poaching and grilling are all wonderful healthy ways of cooking chicken. Even better news – skinless chicken breasts, mini fillets, skinless legs and skinless drumsticks are all cuts that you can eat on a Filling & Healthy day, while if you're counting, chicken is a great choice that is relatively low in **ProPoints** values.

Chicken inspiration

As you do your food shop, it's pretty likely that chicken will make its way into your shopping basket in one form or another, but when you're back in the kitchen it's all too easy to slip into 'autopilot' mode and rely on the same old recipes. This cookbook is here to provide you with fresh ideas, drawing on influences from around the world, as well as looking at new ways with favourite family recipes. From soups, light meals and portable lunches through to prepare-ahead meals and speedy supper solutions, you'll find something to suit every occasion. And with over half of the recipes suitable for a Filling & Healthy day, you'll discover plenty of inspiration no matter where you are on your journey.

WEIGHT WATCHERS
and the ProPoints plan

Food is our fuel, and it's all around us every day. It's time to put yourself back in control of the food choices you make. Weight Watchers gives you a simple, flexible plan to help you achieve this. You can adapt the plan according to your personal preference – whether you want to take a simple approach or a more flexible approach, the choice is yours.

Get the most out of this cookbook

Whether you're on a Filling & Healthy day approach or you've moved to ultimate flexibility and are counting everything, this cookbook will give you inspiring ways to cook chicken no matter where you are on your journey.

Filling & Healthy day ♥

If you see a little green heart beside any of the recipes in this book this means it is suitable if you're on a Filling & Healthy day, so you can cook and eat it confident in the knowledge that you won't need to count anything.

Full flexibility

If you are counting everything you will see on the recipe exactly how many **ProPoints** values you will need to use from your **ProPoints** allowance. This makes it really easy to follow the plan while cooking from scratch as there is no guesswork involved.

Find out more at weightwatchers.co.uk

Quick ProPoints values index

Chicken and red pepper frittata **36**

Really easy chicken satay salad **54**

Super-fast curry **60**

Delicious chicken and ratatouille lasagne **106**

Mediterranean chicken stuffed pittas **30**

Easy quesadillas **32**

Chicken, spinach and feta filo parcels **34**

Chicken and three-bean salad **42**

Cajun chicken and rice **82**

One-pot rosemary and bacon chicken pasta **84**

Tarragon chicken burgers **98**

Gorgeous chicken parmigiana **100**

Easy Tex Mex pasta salad **24**

Zingy chicken fajitas **50**

Chilli chicken spaghetti **58**

Sticky BBQ chicken and wedges **72**

Simple chicken casserole with dumplings **86**

Indian baked chicken with aromatic pilau **90**

Piri piri kebabs **46**

Creamy chicken and mushroom pasta **56**

Baked lemon chicken **70**

Chicken tikka with spiced potatoes **92**

Chicken chilli blanco **94**

Chicken, bacon and sweetcorn pot pies **102**

Classic poule au pot **108**

LIGHT Meals

PROPOINTS VALUES

HOT AND SOUR
Chicken Broth

An Asian-style broth packed with tender chicken and vegetables
– plus aromas and flavours to satisfy all the senses.

ProPoints values per serving **4**
ProPoints values per recipe 7

Serves 2
Takes 15 minutes

600 ml (20 fl oz) chicken stock, made
    from stock cubes or powder
½ red **chilli**, de-seeded and sliced
1 **garlic clove**, sliced
2.5 cm (1 inch) **fresh root ginger**,
    peeled and sliced
1 **lemongrass** stalk, bruised
1 tablespoon Thai fish sauce
100 g (3½ oz) **baby corn**, sliced on
    the diagonal
75 g (2¾ oz) **sugar snap peas**, halved
    on the diagonal
2 x 125 g (4½ oz) **skinless, boneless**
    chicken breasts, sliced thinly
1 tablespoon lime juice
125 g (4½ oz) **beansprouts**, rinsed
fresh coriander sprigs, to serve

1 Place the stock in a lidded saucepan with the chilli, garlic, ginger, lemongrass and fish sauce. Cover the pan and simmer for 5 minutes, then remove the lemongrass.

2 Add the baby corn to the pan and bring back to the boil.

3 Add the sugar snap peas and sliced chicken and simmer for 3 minutes, by which time the chicken should be completely cooked through and the vegetables should be tender but still retain some bite.

4 Add the lime juice to flavour the broth. Divide the beansprouts between 2 deep bowls then ladle the hot and sour broth, chicken and vegetables on top. Serve with the coriander sprigs scattered over the broth.

Cook's tip Bruising the lemongrass helps to release its flavour. Use the flat of a kitchen knife or a rolling pin to crush the stalk, but leaving it in one piece.

HEARTY CHICKEN
Hotchpotch

They say chicken soup is good for the soul, and this filling hotchpotch
is certainly very comforting, as well as being a great value meal.

 ProPoints values per serving
ProPoints values per recipe 14

 Serves 4
Preparation time: 15 minutes
Cooking time: 40 minutes

2 x 165 g (5¾ oz) skinless chicken
    legs
1 chicken stock cube
1 bay leaf
1 onion, sliced thinly
1 celery stick, cubed
2 large carrots, peeled and cubed
200 g (7 oz) potatoes, peeled and
    cubed
salt and freshly ground black pepper
chopped fresh parsley, to serve
    (optional)

1 Place the chicken legs in a large lidded saucepan with the
crumbled stock cube, bay leaf, seasoning and 1.2 litres (2 pints)
cold water. Bring to the boil, then reduce the heat and simmer
gently, covered, for 20 minutes.

2 Add all the vegetables to the pan and continue to cook for
15 minutes. Remove the chicken legs and the bay leaf from the
pan, and leave the vegetables to carry on cooking for 5 minutes
or until tender.

3 Meanwhile, use two forks to shred the cooked chicken from the
bones. Stir the chicken meat back into the pan, along with the
parsley, if using.

4 Ladle into warm bowls to serve.

Cook's tip To skin each chicken leg, grasp the skin at the top of
the leg using kitchen towel and then pull it down and off over the
bony drumstick end. Trim off all visible fat after skinning.

MOROCCAN
Chicken and Chickpea Soup

A wonderfully aromatic soup, this is packed with so many filling foods that it is on its way to being a stew – you certainly won't be left feeling hungry. Great served with a Weight Watchers pitta bread, for an extra 3 *ProPoints* values.

ProPoints values per serving
ProPoints values per recipe 29

Serves 4
Takes 25 minutes

calorie controlled cooking spray
2 red **onions**, chopped finely
1 litre (1¾ pints) chicken stock, made
    from stock cubes or powder
1 tablespoon ground cumin
1 tablespoon ground coriander
½ teaspoon ground cinnamon
½ teaspoon chilli powder
3 tablespoons tomato purée
150 g (5½ oz) **skinless, boneless
    chicken breast**, chopped finely
juice of 1 lemon
2 x 410 g cans **chickpeas**, rinsed
    and drained
60 g (2 oz) **wholewheat couscous**
3 tablespoons chopped **fresh mint**
salt and freshly ground black pepper
fresh flat leaf parsley sprigs,
    to garnish

1 Spray a large lidded saucepan with the cooking spray. Cook the onions, stirring occasionally, for 5 minutes until starting to soften. Add a splash of chicken stock if the onions are catching on the base of the saucepan.

2 Add the spices and tomato purée and cook for 1 minute, stirring, to develop the flavours. Add the chicken and mix well before adding the rest of the stock, the lemon juice and the chickpeas. Cover the pan, bring to the boil and simmer for 10 minutes.

3 Stir the couscous and mint into the soup and re-cover the pan. Leave to stand, off the heat, for 3 minutes or until the couscous is tender. Season to taste. Ladle into warm bowls to serve, garnished with parsley.

Cook's tip You can also use the same amount of **wholewheat giant couscous** if you prefer, for a different texture. Simmer the soup for 10–12 minutes after adding the giant couscous and add the mint just before serving. The *ProPoints* values stay the same.

MISO
Soup Bowl

Japanese ingredients are becoming much more widely available.
This easy noodle soup bowl uses miso as a flavoursome base, and is packed full of
different ingredients for a really filling meal in a bowl.

 ProPoints values per serving
ProPoints values per recipe 15

Serves 2
Takes 15 minutes

200 g (7 oz) **skinless chicken breast
   steaks**
80 g (3 oz) dried udon noodles or
   egg noodles
calorie controlled cooking spray
100 g (3½ oz) chestnut **mushrooms**,
   sliced
2 **carrots**, cut into matchsticks
4 **spring onions**, sliced
2.5 cm (1 inch) **fresh root ginger**,
   peeled and cut into matchsticks
2 x 18 g sachets miso soup paste
   (or 2 tablespoons miso paste
   from a jar)
400 ml (14 fl oz) boiling water
40 g (1½ oz) fresh **spinach**
lime wedges, to serve

1 Griddle or grill the chicken breast steaks for 4–5 minutes on each
side until cooked through.

2 Add the noodles to a pan of boiling water and cook according to
the packet instructions.

3 Meanwhile, spray a large saucepan with the cooking spray and
stir-fry the mushrooms, carrots and spring onions for 3 minutes until
slightly softened and starting to colour. Add the ginger, miso paste
and boiling water, and bring the soup to the boil.

4 Drain the noodles and divide between 2 deep bowls. Add the
spinach leaves and then ladle the hot miso soup and vegetables
on top.

5 Slice the chicken and add to each bowl. Serve with lime wedges
to squeeze into the soup as you eat.

Variation To cut down on preparation time, use a pack of ready-
prepared stir-fry vegetables in place of the mushrooms, carrots,
spring onions and spinach. The **ProPoints** values per serving will
stay the same.

EASY TEX MEX
Pasta Salad

This pasta salad makes a great packed lunch. Add a handful of zero *ProPoints* value salad leaves as an extra if you like.

 9 *ProPoints* values per serving
ProPoints values per recipe 37

 Serves 4
Takes 20 minutes + cooling

1 teaspoon ground cumin
½ teaspoon chilli powder
300 g (10½ oz) skinless chicken
    breast steaks
150 g (5½ oz) dried wholewheat
    pasta
2 tomatoes, chopped
1 red pepper, de-seeded and cubed
198 g can sweetcorn, drained
410 g can mixed beans in water,
    rinsed and drained
½ red chilli, de-seeded and chopped
    finely
zest and juice of ½ lime
3 tablespoons chopped fresh
    coriander
125 g (4½ oz) low fat natural yogurt
salt and freshly ground black pepper
fresh flat leaf parsley sprigs,
    to garnish

1 Preheat the grill. Combine the cumin and chilli powder and rub on to the chicken breast steaks. Grill the chicken for 8–10 minutes, until cooked through. Leave to cool unless you will be serving the salad straight away.

2 Meanwhile, cook the pasta according to the packet instructions.

3 In a large mixing bowl, combine the tomatoes, pepper, sweetcorn, mixed beans and chilli with the lime zest and juice, and 2 tablespoons of the chopped coriander. Season to taste. Stir the remaining coriander into the yogurt in a separate bowl.

4 When the pasta is cooked, drain it and rinse in cold water, then mix together with the other salad ingredients.

5 Slice the cooked chicken and serve on top of the pasta salad, with the coriander yogurt drizzled on top. Garnish with fresh parsley sprigs.

WARM CHICKEN LIVER
and Bacon Salad

Chicken livers are amazing value for money and have a deliciously rich flavour. They pair well with bacon in this robust salad.

ProPoints values per serving
ProPoints values per recipe 12

Serves 2
Takes 15 minutes

1 **Weight Watchers petit pain**, cut into 10 thin slices
1 **garlic clove**, halved
250 g (9 oz) **chicken livers**, defrosted if frozen, rinsed and patted dry
calorie controlled cooking spray
4 **bacon medallions**, snipped
6 **spring onions**, chopped roughly
175 g (6 oz) cherry **tomatoes**, halved
1 tablespoon balsamic vinegar
½ teaspoon grainy mustard
60 g (2 oz) **salad leaves**
salt and freshly ground black pepper

1 Preheat the grill. Rub the slices of petit pain with the halved garlic clove to give a gentle garlicky flavour. Toast for about 1 minute on each side until crisp and golden. Set aside.

2 Preheat a non-stick frying pan. Snip the chicken livers into bite-sized pieces. Spray the frying pan with the cooking spray and stir-fry the livers for 3–4 minutes over a high heat until they are cooked through but still with a touch of pink in the centre. Remove to a plate and wipe out the pan with kitchen towel.

3 Spray the frying pan with more cooking spray and stir-fry the bacon and onions for 2 minutes until starting to colour. Add the cherry tomatoes and cook for 1 minute.

4 Mix the balsamic vinegar and mustard with 1 tablespoon of water to make a dressing. Return the chicken livers to the frying pan with the dressing, remove from the heat, and toss to combine. Season to taste.

5 Serve spooned over the salad leaves, and with the garlic croûtes on the side.

Cook's tip When preparing chicken livers, use a pair of kitchen scissors to snip away any stringy sinews and to chop the livers into more manageable bite-sized morsels.

Variation For another recipe that's suitable if you're on a Filling & Healthy day, toss the warm chicken liver and bacon mixture through a pan of cooked **wholewheat pasta** instead of salad leaves. Add 6 **ProPoints** values per person for a 195 g (7 oz) cooked portion.

QUICK
Curried Chicken Topper

Inspired by the classic favourite, Coronation Chicken, this version is a versatile filler or topper for sandwiches, wraps or a crisp-skinned jacket potato, and perfect if you're on a Filling & Healthy day. Add a zero *ProPoints* value side salad as an accompaniment.

 ProPoints values per serving 3
ProPoints values per recipe 13

 Serves 4
Takes 5 minutes

2 teaspoons lemon juice
1 teaspoon medium curry powder
a pinch of turmeric
1 teaspoon granulated artificial
   sweetener
200 g (7 oz) cooked skinless,
   boneless chicken breast, cubed
300 g pot reduced fat natural
   cottage cheese
100 g (3½ oz) seedless grapes,
   quartered

1 Mix the lemon juice, curry powder, turmeric and sweetener to a paste. Add the chicken and stir to coat in the spice mixture.

2 Add the cottage cheese and grapes and stir gently until combined. The topper is now ready to serve.

Cook's tip Cooking skinless boneless chicken breasts by poaching them ensures that the meat remains deliciously moist. Add the breasts to a pan of boiling chicken stock. Bring the liquid back to the boil, remove the pan from the heat, cover with a lid and leave to stand for 15 minutes, by which time the chicken should be cooked through. Remove from the liquid to cool.

Variation Substitute a de-seeded and cubed red pepper for the grapes.

EASY
Quesadillas

Filled with a zingy home-made salsa, beans, chicken and me ting cheese, there are plenty of flavours going on in these moreish quesadillas. Serve with a zero **ProPoints** value mixed salad on the side.

 ProPoints values per serving
ProPoints values per recipe 32

Serves 4
Takes 25 minutes

3 ripe **tomatoes**, chopped
3 **spring onions**, sliced
juice of ½ lime
3 tablespoons chopped **fresh coriander**
a few shakes of Tabasco sauce
410 g can **mixed bean salad**, rinsed and drained
4 x **Weight Watchers wraps**
80 g (3 oz) reduced fat mature cheese, grated finely
200 g (7 oz) cooked **skinless, boneless chicken breast**, sliced
salt and freshly ground black pepper

1 Make the salsa by combining the tomatoes, spring onions, lime juice and coriander, adding Tabasco sauce and seasoning to taste. Stir in the beans.

2 Lay out the wraps and divide the cheese evenly between them. Spoon the salsa and bean mixture on to half of each wrap; then top with the chicken. Fold each wrap over to give a half moon shape.

3 Preheat a non-stick frying pan. Add two filled wraps to the pan and cook over a medium heat for 2½ minutes on each side, pressing down as they cook, until the outside is golden brown and crisp, and the cheese is melting inside. Keep warm while you cook the remaining two quesadillas.

4 Cut into wedges to serve.

Variations If you're really pressed for time, you can use 8 tablespoons of a ready-made tomato salsa for 8 **ProPoints** values per serving, and you'll have the quesadillas on the table in under 15 minutes.

Make a more child-friendly version by replacing the salsa and bean mixture with a 410g can of baked beans for 8 **ProPoints** values per serving.

CHICKEN, SPINACH AND FETA
Filo Parcels

These crispy filo parcels can be packed for lunch on the go or served straight from the oven with some boiled new potatoes and zero *ProPoints* value green vegetables for a hot main meal.

 ProPoints values per serving **8**
ProPoints values per recipe 34

Serves 4
Preparation time: 25 minutes
  + cooling
Cooking time: 20 minutes

 Freeze before baking

300 g (10½ oz) sweet potatoes, peeled and cut into 2 cm (¾ inch) cubes
calorie controlled cooking spray
a bunch of spring onions, sliced
2 garlic cloves, crushed
150 g (5½ oz) fresh spinach
200 g (7 oz) cooked skinless, boneless chicken breast, shredded
60 g (2 oz) feta, crumbled
4 x 45 g (1½ oz) sheets filo pastry, measuring 50 x 24 cm (20 x 9½ inches), defrosted if frozen
1 tablespoon sesame seeds
salt and freshly ground black pepper

1 Cook the sweet potatoes in boiling water for 7–8 minutes or until tender, then drain.

2 Meanwhile, spray a frying pan with the cooking spray and fry the spring onions and garlic for 2 minutes. Add the spinach and cook until the leaves have wilted and the excess liquid has evaporated.

3 Mix the garlicky spinach with the sweet potatoes, chicken, feta and seasoning. Spread the filling on a plate to cool. Preheat the oven to Gas Mark 6/200°C/fan oven 180°C.

4 Cut each sheet of filo pastry into two long strips. Spray with the cooking spray and then spoon one eighth of the filling on to the top of each strip. Fold the top left corner down diagonally to meet the right hand side of the pastry, making a small triangular shape. Flip the triangle over and over down the length of the pastry to fully enclose the filling. Repeat to make a total of 8 parcels.

5 Place the parcels on a baking tray, spray with more cooking spray and sprinkle with the sesame seeds.

6 Bake the parcels for 20 minutes until golden brown and crisp. Serve warm or cold.

CHICKEN AND RED PEPPER
Frittata

This frittata is best served at room temperature – add a tomato and basil salad, drizzled with a little balsamic vinegar. It makes a fabulous packed lunch if you're bored with sandwiches.

 ProPoints values per serving **7**
ProPoints values per recipe 27

 Serves 4
Takes 30 minutes

300 g (10½ oz) new potatoes, quartered
calorie controlled cooking spray
2 x 125 g (4½ oz) skinless, boneless chicken breasts, cubed
2 red peppers, de-seeded and cubed
a bunch of spring onions, sliced thickly
100 g (3½ oz) frozen peas
6 eggs
salt and freshly ground black pepper

1 Add the potatoes to a pan of boiling water and simmer for around 10 minutes or until tender.

2 Meanwhile, spray a 28 cm (11 inch) non-stick frying pan with the cooking spray. Stir-fry the chicken and peppers for 4–5 minutes over a high heat until the chicken is cooked through.

3 Add the spring onions and peas and cook for 2 minutes, stirring.

4 Beat the eggs with 2 tablespoons of cold water in a mixing bowl. Season. Drain the potatoes and tip into the egg mixture, along with the frying pan contents. Stir gently to combine.

5 Preheat the grill. Use kitchen towel to wipe out the frying pan, then spray with the cooking spray again. Add the frittata mixture to the pan and cook over a low to medium heat for 10 minutes or until nearly set, gently loosening the edge of the frittata from the pan.

6 Pop the frying pan under the grill (protecting the pan handle from the heat if necessary) and cook for 3–5 minutes until the top is golden brown.

7 Serve the frittata cut into wedges.

QUICK *Dishes*

PROPOINTS VALUES

PIRI PIRI
Kebabs

These kebabs can be cooked under the grill or on the barbecue for a summer lunch.
Serve with a crisp zero *ProPoints* value salad on the side.

 ProPoints values per serving
ProPoints values per recipe 40

 Serves 4
Takes 20 minutes

200 g (7 oz) dried brown basmati
   rice
1 large garlic clove, crushed
¼ teaspoon chilli powder
1 teaspoon paprika
½ teaspoon dried oregano
¼ teaspoon dried thyme
1 tablespoon red wine vinegar or
   lemon juice
500 g (1 lb 2 oz) ready-cubed
   skinless, boneless chicken breasts
1 red pepper, de-seeded and
   chopped roughly
1 yellow pepper, de-seeded and
   chopped roughly
calorie controlled cooking spray
198 g can sweetcorn
150 g (5½ oz) 0% fat natural Greek
   yogurt
fresh flat leaf parsley, to garnish

1 Add the rice to a pan of boiling water and cook according to the packet instructions. Preheat the grill and line the grill pan with foil.

2 Combine the garlic, spices, dried herbs and vinegar or lemon juice in a mixing bowl and toss the chicken in the mixture to coat.

3 Thread the chicken and peppers on to 4 skewers. Spray with the cooking spray and grill for 12 minutes or until the chicken is cooked through, turning the kebabs occasionally.

4 When the rice is tender, stir in the sweetcorn and allow it to heat through for 1 minute. Drain and divide the rice between 4 plates.

5 Add a kebab to each plate, drizzling any cooking juices from the grill pan over the top. Garnish with fresh parsley and serve with the yogurt.

Cook's tips If you like your food fairly spicy, increase the chilli powder to ½ teaspoon to give this recipe a bit more of a kick.

When using wooden skewers, soak them first in cold water for about 30 minutes, to stop them from burning under the grill.

ZINGY
Chicken Fajitas

A fresh, citrus-flavoured version of the Tex-Mex classic – this is a great hands-on, help-yourself meal.

ProPoints values per serving **9**
ProPoints values per recipe 37

Serves 4
Takes 20 minutes

zest of ½ orange
zest and juice of 1 lime
1 teaspoon coriander seeds, crushed
a pinch of chilli flakes
500 g (1 lb 2 oz) skinless chicken
    mini fillets
calorie controlled cooking spray
1 red onion, sliced
3 mixed peppers, de-seeded and
    sliced
1 courgette, cut into batons
8 Weight Watchers tortillas
150 g (5½ oz) 0% fat natural Greek
    yogurt
salt and freshly ground black pepper

1 Combine the orange zest, lime zest and juice, crushed coriander seeds, chilli flakes and seasoning in a bowl. Toss the chicken mini fillets in the mixture to coat.

2 Preheat a large non-stick frying pan on the hob and spray with the cooking spray. Stir-fry the chicken over a high heat for 5 minutes or until cooked through. Remove to a plate and keep warm.

3 Wipe out the pan with kitchen towel and spray with more cooking spray. Fry the onion for 2 minutes before adding the peppers and courgette. Stir-fry for 4 minutes or until the vegetables have taken on some colour and are starting to soften but still retain some bite. Return the chicken to the pan and mix everything together.

4 Warm the tortillas according to the packet instructions.

5 To serve, spread each tortilla with a spoonful of yogurt, pile on some of the chicken fajita mixture and roll it up.

REALLY EASY CHICKEN SATAY
Salad

This is a great recipe to serve when friends come for supper – it's quick to prepare and tastes fantastic. You can prepare the satay sauce and salad ingredients ahead of time, but don't dress the salad until the last minute to keep its lovely crunchy texture.

 ProPoints values per serving
ProPoints values per recipe 26

Serves 4
Takes 20 minutes

4 x 125 g (4½ oz) skinless, boneless
   chicken breasts

For the satay sauce
60 g (2 oz) crunchy peanut butter
2 tablespoons Thai sweet chilli sauce
1 tablespoon dark soy sauce
1 tablespoon lime juice

For the salad
2 carrots, peeled
1 Little Gem lettuce, shredded
125 g (4½ oz) beansprouts
100 g (3½ oz) mange tout, sliced
2 teaspoons sesame seeds, toasted

1 Preheat the grill. Grill the chicken breasts on one side for 6 minutes initially.

2 Meanwhile, combine the peanut butter, chilli sauce, soy sauce and lime juice in a small bowl. Divide the mixture in half.

3 Turn the chicken breasts and grill for a further 3 minutes. Drizzle half of the satay sauce over the chicken and grill for a further 3 minutes.

4 Use a vegetable peeler to shave the carrot into ribbons; toss them together with the remaining salad ingredients. Add 1 tablespoon of cold water to the reserved satay sauce to make a dressing and use this to coat the crunchy salad.

5 Divide the salad between 4 bowls and serve with the hot, sliced grilled satay chicken breasts. Sprinkle with sesame seeds.

CHICKEN
in a Tomato and Chorizo Sauce

A little chorizo goes a long way here, adding real depth of flavour to this Spanish-inspired dish. Mashed potato makes a great accompaniment to help mop up the scrumptious sauce – add 3 *ProPoints* values per person for a 150 g (5½ oz) portion.

ProPoints values per serving 5
ProPoints values per recipe 18

Serves 4
Takes 20 minutes

calorie controlled cooking spray
4 x 125 g (4½ oz) skinless, boneless
   chicken breasts, cut into large
   chunks
75 g (2¾ oz) ready-cubed cooking
   chorizo
1 red pepper, de-seeded and
   chopped roughly
1 yellow pepper, de-seeded and
   chopped roughly
2 garlic cloves, crushed
400 g can chopped tomatoes
fresh thyme sprigs, to garnish

1 Heat a deep non-stick frying pan or sauté pan and spray with the cooking spray. Brown the chicken for 5 minutes, then remove to a plate.

2 Fry the chorizo, peppers and garlic together for 3 minutes, stirring occasionally, until the peppers start to caramelise.

3 Add the tomatoes to the pan and bring to a simmer. Return the chicken to the pan and simmer, uncovered, for 10 minutes. Serve garnished with sprigs of thyme.

ONE-POT
Meals

PROPOINTS VALUES

ONE-DISH MIDWEEK
Roast Chicken

Sage adds a typical 'Sunday roast' flavour to this all-in-one recipe that is perfect for when you're on a Filling & Healthy day, combining wintry root vegetables, chicken and bacon.

ProPoints values per serving
ProPoints values per recipe 22

Serves 4
Preparation time: 15 minutes
Cooking time: 40 minutes

500 g (1 lb 2 oz) **butternut squash**, peeled, de-seeded and cut into chunks
4 **parsnips**, peeled and cut into chunks
2 red **onions**, quartered through the root
4 **garlic cloves**, unpeeled
½ teaspoon dried sage
calorie controlled cooking spray
4 large **fresh sage** leaves (optional)
4 x 125 g (4½ oz) **skinless, boneless chicken breasts**
4 **bacon medallions**
salt and freshly ground black pepper

1 Preheat the oven to Gas Mark 6/200°C/fan oven 180°C.

2 In a large roasting tin, toss the chunks of butternut squash, parsnips, red onions and the garlic cloves with the dried sage and seasoning. Spray with the cooking spray. Roast in the oven for 20 minutes on a high shelf.

3 Meanwhile, place a sage leaf, if using, on top of each chicken breast, and place a bacon medallion over each chicken breast, securing with cocktail sticks or small skewers. Spray with the cooking spray.

4 When the 20 minutes are up, give the vegetables a good stir around and then tuck the chicken breasts into the tin among the vegetables. Cook for 20 minutes or until the chicken is cooked through and the vegetables are starting to caramelise at the edges.

5 Divide between 4 plates to serve.

CARIBBEAN CHICKEN
Hotpot

This wonderfully fragrant and fresh-tasting hotpot takes its inspiration from the sunny Caribbean.

 ProPoints values per serving
ProPoints values per recipe 24

 Serves 4
Preparation time: 15 minutes
Cooking time: 20 minutes

calorie controlled cooking spray
4 x 125 g (4½ oz) skinless, boneless
    chicken breasts
1 onion, chopped roughly
2 garlic cloves, crushed
2.5 cm (1 inch) fresh root ginger,
    peeled and grated
1 teaspoon ground coriander
½ teaspoon ground allspice
½ teaspoon ground cinnamon
¼ teaspoon cayenne pepper
½ teaspoon dried thyme
400 g (14 oz) sweet potatoes, peeled
    and cubed
300 ml (10 fl oz) chicken stock, made
    from stock cubes or powder
1 tablespoon red wine vinegar
200 g (7 oz) green beans, trimmed
    and halved
250 g (9 oz) cherry tomatoes, halved

1 Spray a lidded flameproof casserole with the cooking spray. Brown the chicken breasts for 2 minutes on each side and remove to a plate.

2 Stir-fry the onion in the casserole for 3 minutes then add the garlic, ginger, spices and thyme. Cook for 1 minute, stirring.

3 Add the sweet potatoes to the casserole along with the stock and vinegar. Return the chicken to the casserole and cook, covered, for 10 minutes.

4 Add the green beans and cherry tomatoes to the casserole, pushing them down into the liquid. Cook, covered, for a further 10 minutes or until the green beans are tender.

5 Serve the hotpot in deep bowls.

Cook's tip Allspice is an individual spice (unlike mixed spice) that is much used in Caribbean cooking, where it is also known as Jamaican pepper or pimento. Its taste has been described as a combination of cinnamon, cloves, nutmeg and pepper.

SMOKY ROAST CHICKEN
and Vegetables

If you're looking for a new way to serve roast chicken, try this delicious recipe – smoked paprika, cumin and lemon add plenty of flavour to the chicken and vegetables.

ProPoints values per serving **6**
ProPoints values per recipe 52

Serves 4 with leftovers
Preparation time: 20 minutes
Cooking time: 1 hour 20 minutes

1.4 kg (3 lb) whole chicken
1 teaspoon smoked paprika
2 teaspoons ground cumin
3 tablespoons lemon juice
1 head garlic, unpeeled
calorie controlled cooking spray
1 aubergine, chopped roughly
3 courgettes, sliced thickly
1 butternut squash, peeled,
  de-seeded and chopped roughly
200 g (7 oz) 0% fat natural Greek
  yogurt
salt and freshly ground black pepper

1 Preheat the oven to Gas Mark 5/190°C/fan oven 170°C.

2 Start by removing the skin from the chicken. Gently lift the skin away from the chicken and use kitchen scissors to snip down the length of the breastbone and then down the backbone, without cutting into the flesh. Grasping the skin with kitchen towel, pull it off and over the leg and wing on each side. Trim off any excess fat and tie the legs together. Place the chicken in a large roasting tin and cut slashes in the breast and legs using a kitchen knife.

3 Mix the smoked paprika and cumin with the lemon juice and pour this all over the chicken. Cut the head of garlic in half horizontally and nestle the two halves next to the chicken. Spray the chicken and garlic with the cooking spray and cover loosely with foil. Bake in the oven for 20 minutes.

4 Meanwhile, toss the aubergine, courgettes and squash together and spray with the cooking spray. Season and set aside.

5 When the 20 minutes are up, baste the chicken. Add the vegetables to the roasting tin around the chicken, replace the foil and cook for 15 minutes.

6 The garlic should now be tender; remove it from the roasting tin and leave to cool. Give the vegetables a stir and roast the chicken and vegetables for a further 30 minutes. After 30 minutes, check that the chicken is cooked by piercing the thickest part of the leg; the juices should run clear. Remove the chicken to a serving dish, cover and keep warm. Continue to cook the veg for a further 15 minutes, without the foil, until soft and slightly caramelised.

7 Meanwhile, squeeze the cooked garlic from its papery skin into a bowl and mash to a paste. Stir in the Greek yogurt, ready to serve. Carve the chicken and serve 125 g (4½ oz) cooked chicken per person, accompanied by the roast vegetables and garlicky yogurt.

CAJUN CHICKEN
and Rice

Don't be put off by the length of the ingredients list in this recipe: the first five ingredients combine to make a Cajun spice mix in a matter of seconds, to give this hearty dish a robust flavour.

 ProPoints values per serving
ProPoints values per recipe 33

 Serves 4
Preparation time: 15 minutes
Cooking time: 40 minutes

½ tablespoon ground cumin
½ tablespoon ground coriander
½ tablespoon paprika
½ teaspoon dried oregano
¼ teaspoon cayenne pepper
1 garlic clove, crushed
juice of 1 lime
4 x 125 g (4½ oz) skinless, boneless
    chicken breasts
calorie controlled cooking spray
1 onion, chopped roughly
1 yellow pepper, de-seeded and
    chopped roughly
1 green pepper, de-seeded and
    chopped roughly
150 g (5½ oz) chestnut mushrooms,
    chopped roughly
200 g (7 oz) dried brown basmati
    rice
200 g (7 oz) cherry tomatoes,
    quartered
600 ml (20 fl oz) chicken stock, made
    from stock cubes or powder
lime wedges, to serve

1 Preheat the oven to Gas Mark 6/200°C/fan oven 180°C.

2 Make the spice mix by simply combining the first five ingredients together in a small bowl. Reserve half the spice mix for the rice, then stir the rest with the garlic and lime juice to make a paste. Rub this into the chicken breasts and set aside, covered, in the fridge.

3 Spray a lidded flameproof casserole with the cooking spray and fry the onion for 3 minutes. Add the peppers and mushrooms and cook for 3 minutes, stirring occasionally.

4 Add the rest of the spice mixture and the rice and cook for 1 minute, stirring. Mix in the tomatoes and pour in the stock. Bring to the boil, stir the rice once, then pop the lid on and put in the oven to cook for 20 minutes.

5 Place the chicken breasts on top of the rice in the casserole (there's no need to stir the rice), replace the lid and cook for 20 minutes or until the chicken is cooked through.

6 Serve the Cajun rice and chicken on warm plates with lime wedges to squeeze over.

Variation Increase the veg content by adding a couple of roughly chopped courgettes in step 3.

ONE-POT
Rosemary and Bacon Chicken Pasta

There's very little washing up with this one-pot pasta dish. Instead of cooking the sauce and pasta separately, everything is cooked together, giving a really rich and flavoursome result. Serve with a zero *ProPoints* value leafy salad on the side.

ProPoints values per serving
ProPoints values per recipe 32

Serves 4
Preparation time: 15 minutes
Cooking time: 20 minutes

calorie controlled cooking spray
4 bacon medallions, chopped
1 red onion, chopped roughly
400 g (14 oz) ready-cubed skinless,
  boneless chicken breast
150 g (5½ oz) closed cap
  mushrooms, chopped roughly
2 garlic cloves, crushed
½ teaspoon smoked paprika
400 g can chopped tomatoes
1½ teaspoons dried rosemary
200 g (7 oz) dried wholewheat pasta
900 ml (1½ pints) chicken stock,
  made from stock cubes or powder
a few dashes of Worcestershire sauce
salt and freshly ground black pepper
chopped fresh parsley, to garnish

1 Heat a large saucepan or flameproof casserole and spray with the cooking spray. Brown the bacon and onion together for 2 minutes before adding the chicken and cooking for another 2 minutes, stirring. Next, add the mushrooms and garlic and cook for a further 2 minutes.

2 Mix in the smoked paprika, tomatoes and rosemary, then add the pasta, stock, Worcestershire sauce and seasoning. Bring to the boil and simmer for 20 minutes or until the pasta is tender and has absorbed the excess liquid, leaving it coated in a rich tomato sauce.

3 Garnish with chopped parsley and serve straight from the pot, ladled into warm bowls.

SIMPLE CHICKEN CASSEROLE
with Dumplings

A comforting casserole that's sure to find favour with the whole family,
particularly on a cold winter's day.

 ProPoints values per serving
ProPoints values per recipe 37

Serves 4
Preparation time: 20 minutes
Cooking time: 30 minutes

calorie controlled cooking spray
4 x 125 g (4½ oz) **skinless, boneless chicken breasts**
2 **leeks**, sliced thickly
4 large **carrots**, sliced thickly
400 g (14 oz) new **potatoes**, halved
3 **fresh thyme** sprigs (or 1 teaspoon dried thyme)
1 tablespoon plain flour
500 ml (18 fl oz) chicken stock, made from stock cubes or powder
200 g (7 oz) Savoy **cabbage**, shredded coarsely
salt and freshly ground black pepper

For the dumplings
100 g (3½ oz) self-raising flour
50 g (1¾ oz) low fat spread

1 Spray a flameproof casserole with the cooking spray and brown the chicken breasts. Transfer them to a plate once golden brown.

2 Add the leeks, carrots and potatoes to the casserole and cook for 2 minutes, stirring. Mix in the thyme, flour, seasoning and chicken stock. Bring to the boil and rest the chicken breasts on top of the vegetables.

3 Simmer, covered, for 10 minutes. Meanwhile, rub the self-raising flour and low fat spread together until crumb-like and set aside for the dumplings.

4 Add the cabbage to the casserole, pressing it down into the liquid. Add just enough water to the dumpling mixture to bring it together as a soft but not sticky dough. Shape into 8 dumplings and drop these into the casserole, making sure that they are in contact with the liquid.

5 Pop the lid back on the casserole and cook for 15 minutes until the dumplings are plump and fluffy and the vegetables are tender.

6 Divide the casserole between 4 warm shallow bowls to serve.

COMFORT
Food

PROPOINTS VALUES

INDIAN BAKED CHICKEN
with Aromatic Pilau

Baking the chicken breasts in a foil parcel seals in all the flavours, and creates delicious cooking juices to drizzle over the rice. Serve with a pile of green beans for no extra *ProPoints* values.

 9 *ProPoints* values per serving
ProPoints values per recipe 34

Serves 4
Preparation time: 15 minutes
Cooking time: 25 minutes

1 green chilli, de-seeded and
    chopped finely
1 garlic clove, crushed
2.5 cm (1 inch) fresh root ginger,
    grated
3 tablespoons chopped fresh
    coriander
a pinch of ground turmeric
100 g (3½ oz) low fat natural yogurt
4 x 125 g (4½ oz) skinless, boneless
    chicken breasts

For the pilau
calorie controlled cooking spray
1 onion, chopped finely
2 teaspoons cumin seeds
4 cardamom seeds, crushed
1 cinnamon stick
1 bay leaf
200 g (7 oz) dried brown basmati
    rice
500 ml (18 fl oz) boiling water

To garnish (optional)
grated lemon zest
fresh coriander sprigs

1 Preheat the oven to Gas Mark 5/190°C/fan oven 170°C.

2 To make the pilau, spray a large lidded pan with the cooking spray and cook the onion for 4 minutes, stirring, until starting to colour and soften.

3 Add the spices, bay leaf and rice and cook for 1 minute, stirring. Pour in the water and bring back to the boil. Give the rice a stir, cover the pan and reduce the heat to its lowest setting. Leave to cook, undisturbed, for 25 minutes.

4 Meanwhile, mix the chilli, garlic, ginger, coriander and turmeric with the yogurt to make a spicy paste.

5 Cut 4 large squares of foil, spray each one with the cooking spray and place a chicken breast in the centre. Spoon the yogurt-spice paste on to each one and seal the edges of the foil parcel, leaving room for air to circulate inside the parcels. Place on a baking tray and bake in the oven for 20 minutes.

6 Remove the whole spices from the pilau rice before serving. Open the chicken parcels at the table to enjoy the fragrant aromas. Drizzle the juices from the parcels over the pilau to serve. Garnish with grated lemon zest and coriander sprigs, if liked.

CHICKEN TIKKA
with Spiced Potatoes

Marinating the chicken in a spiced yogurt mixture adds plenty of flavour and helps ensure the meat will be tender and juicy. You could serve the chicken and crispy potatoes with some green beans, or with a crunchy mixed salad.

 ProPoints values per serving
ProPoints values per recipe 41

 Serves 4
Preparation time: 15 minutes +
   minimum 30 minutes marinating
Cooking time: 30 minutes

4 x 165 g (5¾ oz) **skinless, boneless chicken breasts**
900 g (2 lb) unpeeled **potatoes**
½ teaspoon turmeric
calorie controlled cooking spray
2 teaspoons cumin seeds
1 teaspoon black onion seeds

For the marinade
1 tablespoon lemon juice
1 **garlic clove**, crushed
2.5 cm (1 inch) **fresh root ginger**, grated
1 tablespoon tomato purée
½ teaspoon turmeric
1½ teaspoons ground cumin
1½ teaspoons ground coriander
¼ teaspoon chilli powder
150 g (5½ oz) **fat-free natural yogurt**

To garnish
thinly sliced red **onion**
chopped green **chilli**
fresh coriander sprigs
lime wedges

1 Cut slashes in each chicken breast to allow the flavour of the marinade to penetrate. Make the marinade by mixing together the lemon juice, garlic, ginger, tomato purée and spices, then blend in the yogurt. Turn the chicken breasts in the spiced yogurt to coat them. Cover and leave to marinate in the fridge for at least 30 minutes and up to 24 hours.

2 Preheat the oven to Gas Mark 7/220°C/fan oven 200°C, with a large baking tray on the top shelf.

3 Cube the potatoes and cook them in boiling water, with the turmeric added, for 5 minutes or until the edges are beginning to soften. Drain, then shake them in the lidded pan to slightly roughen up the edges. Tip out on to the hot baking tray and spray with the cooking spray. Sprinkle the seeds over the potatoes and bake them on the top shelf for 30 minutes, stirring halfway through the cooking time.

4 Meanwhile, remove the chicken tikka breasts from the marinade and place in a roasting tin. Cook in the oven for 20 minutes, below the potatoes.

5 Serve the crispy spiced potatoes with the chicken tikka. Garnish with red onion, green chilli, coriander and lime wedges.

Variation Use 4 x 200 g (7 oz) **skinless chicken legs** instead. Skin the legs (see Cook's tip on page 16) and slash them before marinating. Chicken legs take longer to cook, so put them in the oven at the same time as the potatoes in step 3. The **ProPoints** values per person will be 12.

CHICKEN CHILLI
Blanco

We're all familiar with chilli con carne, but this white chilli, made with chicken and without tomatoes, makes a welcome change. The flavour is fragrant rather than spicy; if you want more chilli heat simply add a few shakes of Tabasco sauce.

 ProPoints values per serving 10
ProPoints values per recipe 42

 Serves 4
Takes 30 minutes

 Freeze chilli only

calorie controlled cooking spray
2 **onions**, chopped
2 **celery** sticks, chopped
3 **garlic cloves**, crushed
1 green **chilli**, de-seeded and sliced
450 ml (16 fl oz) chicken stock, made from stock cubes or powder
1 tablespoon ground cumin
1 teaspoon smoked paprika
500 g (1 lb 2 oz) ready-cubed skinless, boneless **chicken breasts**
410 g can **haricot beans**, rinsed and drained
100 g (3½ oz) **0% fat natural Greek yogurt**
salt and freshly ground black pepper
fresh **coriander** sprigs, to garnish
8 **Weight Watchers tortillas**, to serve

For the salsa
2 ripe **tomatoes**, chopped
½ green **chilli**, de-seeded and sliced
juice of ½ lime
½ red **onion**, chopped finely
½ red **pepper**, de-seeded and diced

1 Spray a large lidded saucepan or flameproof casserole with the cooking spray. Fry the onions, celery, garlic and green chilli for 2 minutes, stirring. Add 6 tablespoons of the stock and cook, covered, for 5 minutes until softened.

2 Stir in the spices, seasoning and the chicken and cook, stirring, for 2 minutes before adding the rest of the stock and the beans. Simmer, partially covered, for 20 minutes.

3 While the chilli is cooking, combine the tomatoes, green chilli, lime juice, red onion and red pepper in a bowl to make the salsa. Set aside.

4 Ladle the chilli blanco into deep bowls and top with the salsa and yogurt. Garnish with coriander sprigs and serve with the tortillas.

MUST-TRY
Asian-Inspired Meatballs

These meatballs are especially good served with brown rice, but if you're in a hurry, wholewheat couscous is very quick to prepare. Add your favourite vegetables, such as red pepper and steamed broccoli, without adding *ProPoints* values.

 ProPoints values per serving
ProPoints values per recipe 14

 Serves 4
Takes 25 minutes

1 green **pepper**, de-seeded and quartered
1 **egg white**
1 teaspoon ground ginger
2 **garlic cloves**, crushed
4 tablespoons dark soy sauce
500 g (1 lb 2 oz) **skinless, boneless chicken breasts**, chopped very finely
calorie controlled cooking spray
2 tablespoons cider vinegar
2 teaspoons granulated artificial sweetener
a bunch of **spring onions**, sliced
225 g can **water chestnuts**, drained and sliced

1 Add the green pepper to a pan of boiling water and cook for 8 minutes until softened. Drain, refresh in cold water and chop into small pieces.

2 Meanwhile, mix the egg white, ginger, garlic and 1 tablespoon of the soy sauce together. Add the chicken and the chopped green pepper and stir gently to combine.

3 Spray a large non-stick frying pan with the cooking spray. Use a tablespoon measure to portion the mixture into 24 meatballs, putting them directly into the frying pan. Fry for 8–10 minutes, turning occasionally, until browned and cooked through. Remove the meatballs to a plate and keep warm.

4 Combine the rest of the soy sauce with the cider vinegar, sweetener and 125 ml (4 fl oz) water and pour this into the frying pan. Boil for 3–4 minutes until slightly reduced.

5 Add the spring onions and water chestnuts to the sauce, then return the meatballs to the pan. Toss them in the sauce to glaze before serving.

Cook's tips If you use a food processor to chop the chicken, you will get a smoother texture to your meatballs than if you chop the chicken by hand. Be careful not to over-process the meat, however, or the meatballs will have a bouncy texture.

When forming the meatballs, dip the tablespoon measure into a bowl of cold water occasionally to stop the mixture sticking to it.

Variation Replace the chicken breasts with the same amount of **turkey breast mince** for a slightly different flavour. They will be 4 *ProPoints* values per person.

TARRAGON
Chicken Burgers

Tarragon and lemon add real depth of flavour to these easy burgers.

ProPoints values per serving **8**
ProPoints values per recipe 33

Serves 4
Takes 20 minutes

 Freeze before grilling

2 slices **Weight Watchers brown Danish bread**
2 tablespoons **skimmed milk**
1 teaspoon **grainy mustard**
1 **garlic clove**, crushed
zest of 1 lemon
3 tablespoons chopped **fresh tarragon**
500 g (1 lb 2 oz) **skinless, boneless chicken breasts**
calorie controlled cooking spray
4 tablespoons **light mayonnaise**
50 g (1¾ oz) **0% fat natural Greek yogurt**
4 **brown sandwich thins**
salt and freshly ground black pepper

To serve
3 **tomatoes**, sliced
40 g (1½ oz) wild **rocket**

1 Preheat the grill.

2 Whizz the bread to crumbs, either in a food processor or using a hand-held blender. Put them in a bowl with the milk, mustard, garlic, half of the lemon zest, seasoning and 2 tablespoons of the chopped tarragon. Mix together.

3 Finely chop the chicken breast meat, either in a food processor or by hand, using a large kitchen knife. Combine the chopped chicken with the flavoured crumb mixture and mix well.

4 Shape into 4 x 10 cm (4 inch) burgers – wet your hands first to stop the mixture sticking to them.

5 Spray the burgers with the cooking spray and grill for 10 minutes, or until cooked through, turning once.

6 Meanwhile, combine the mayonnaise and Greek yogurt with the rest of the lemon zest and tarragon. Lightly toast the unsplit sandwich thins, then pull them apart and spread the lemon and tarragon mayo inside.

7 Fill each sandwich thin with some sliced tomato, a chicken and tarragon burger, and some wild rocket. Serve immediately.

Cook's tip If you can't get fresh tarragon, replace it with 3 teaspoons of dried tarragon, rehydrating it first in a little boiling water, to bring out the flavour.

Variation Replace the chicken breasts with the same amount of **turkey breast mince** if you prefer. The **ProPoints** values will be 9 per serving.

GORGEOUS CHICKEN
Parmigiana

With gooey melting mozzarella and a Parmesan crust, this dish feels utterly indulgent. Wonderful served with sugar snap peas and some crispy oven-sautéed potatoes (see Cook's tip, below).

 8 *ProPoints* values per serving
ProPoints values per recipe 30

Serves 4
Preparation time: 15 minutes
Cooking time: 25 minutes

3 slices **Weight Watchers brown Danish bread**
50 g (1¾ oz) Parmesan cheese, grated finely
125 g (4½ oz) **low fat natural yogurt**
4 x 125 g (4½ oz) **skinless chicken breast steaks**
calorie controlled cooking spray
500 g carton **passata**
1 **garlic clove**, crushed
½ teaspoon dried mixed herbs
zest of ½ lemon
1 teaspoon granulated artificial sweetener
½ chicken stock cube, crumbled
125 g ball mozzarella light cheese, drained and cut into 8 slices
salt and freshly ground black pepper
fresh basil leaves, to garnish

1 Preheat the oven to Gas Mark 7/220°C/200°C fan oven, with a baking tray on the top shelf.

2 Whizz the bread to crumbs in a mini food processor or using a hand-held blender. Combine with two thirds of the Parmesan and tip the mixture on to a plate. Pour the yogurt into a bowl.

3 Dip each chicken breast steak in the yogurt followed by the Parmesan crumbs, to coat both sides.

4 Spray the preheated baking tray with the cooking spray and place the crumbed chicken steaks on the hot tray. Spray them with the cooking spray and bake in the oven for 15 minutes until crisp and golden brown, turning the chicken steaks over halfway through.

5 Meanwhile, simmer the passata with the garlic, herbs, lemon zest, sweetener, chicken stock cube and seasoning in an uncovered saucepan for 5 minutes, and leave the mozzarella to drain on a double layer of kitchen towel, to absorb some of the excess liquid.

6 Pour the tomato sauce into a 23 cm (9 inch) square baking dish, or 4 small individual baking dishes. Add the crisp chicken steaks and nestle the mozzarella slices in between the chicken. Scatter with the rest of the Parmesan cheese.

7 Bake in the oven for 10 minutes until the sauce is bubbling and the cheese is melted and golden brown. Garnish with the fresh basil leaves and serve.

Cook's tip For crispy oven-sautéed potatoes, cube 4 x 225 g (8 oz) baking **potatoes** and parboil them for 5 minutes; drain, then spray with cooking spray and roast on a baking tray for 25–30 minutes, for an additional 5 *ProPoints* values per person.

CHICKEN, BACON AND SWEETCORN
Pot Pies

Do your flour-based sauces tend to turn out lumpy? Then give this recipe a whirl – the simple sauce is made by combining soft cheese and stock. Serve with zero *ProPoints* value carrots and cabbage.

 ProPoints values per serving
ProPoints values per recipe 39

Serves 4
Preparation time: 25 minutes
Cooking time: 20 minutes

 Freeze before baking

600 g (1 lb 5 oz) potatoes, peeled
   and cubed
2 tablespoons chopped fresh chives
calorie controlled cooking spray
500 g (1 lb 2 oz) ready-cubed
   skinless, boneless chicken breasts
4 bacon medallions, chopped
198 g can sweetcorn, drained
150 g (5½ oz) low fat soft cheese
150 ml (5 fl oz) chicken stock, made
   from stock cubes or powder
salt and freshly ground black pepper

1 Preheat the oven to Gas Mark 6/200°C/fan oven 180°C.

2 Cook the potatoes in boiling water for 15 minutes or until tender. Drain and mash, adding the chopped chives.

3 Meanwhile, spray a non-stick frying pan with the cooking spray and stir-fry the chicken and bacon for 5 minutes over a high heat.

4 Remove the pan from the heat and add the sweetcorn. Divide the mixture between four 300 ml (10 fl oz) capacity ovenproof pie dishes or bowls (or you can use one larger dish with a 1.2 litre (2 pint) capacity).

5 Place the soft cheese in a mixing bowl and stir to soften it. Gradually whisk in the stock to make a smooth sauce. Season and divide between the pie dishes.

6 Spoon the mashed potatoes on top of each dish and spray with the cooking spray. Place the pie dishes on a baking tray and bake in the oven for 20 minutes until the sauce is bubbling and the potato top is golden and crisp.

Cook's tip You can significantly cut down the preparation time for this recipe by cooking extra potatoes if you're having potatoes for dinner the previous day. You'll need an extra 600 g (1 lb 5 oz), mashed without adding any milk or fat.

STUFFED CHICKEN BREASTS
with Roasted Vegetables

An easy prepare-ahead dish perfect for dinner with friends. Serve with 150 g (5½ oz) baby new potatoes for an extra 3 **ProPoints** values per person.

 ProPoints values per serving **5**
ProPoints values per recipe 19

 Serves 4
Preparation time: 20 minutes
Cooking time: 25–30 minutes

calorie controlled cooking spray
150 g (5½ oz) spinach
3 garlic cloves, crushed
2 courgettes, sliced into half moons
250 g (9 oz) cherry tomatoes, halved
1 teaspoon fresh thyme leaves
100 g (3½ oz) quark
a pinch of grated nutmeg
4 x 125 g (4½ oz) skinless, boneless
   chicken breasts
4 x 25 g (1 oz) slices premium ham
salt and freshly ground black pepper

1 Preheat the oven to Gas Mark 6/200°C/fan oven 180°C.

2 Spray a non-stick frying pan with the cooking spray and cook the spinach with 2 of the crushed garlic cloves until wilted and quite dry. Tip the spinach out on to a chopping board, chop roughly and spread it out on a plate to cool.

3 Toss the courgettes and cherry tomatoes together with the thyme and the remaining garlic on a large baking tray. Season and spray with the cooking spray.

4 Season the quark with a little nutmeg and mix in the spinach. Cut a deep horizontal pocket in each chicken breast and spoon in a quarter of the stuffing. Wrap a slice of ham around each stuffed chicken breast and add to the tray with the vegetables. Spray with cooking spray.

5 Bake the chicken and vegetables for 25–30 minutes, until the vegetables are tender and the chicken breasts are cooked through.

DELICIOUS CHICKEN
and Ratatouille Lasagne

Lasagne is an ever-popular dish to feed a crowd, and this chicken version also features a flavoursome ratatouille sauce. Serve with a large leafy salad topped with shaved carrot ribbons, for no extra *ProPoints* values.

 7 *ProPoints* values per serving
ProPoints values per recipe 41

 Serves 6
Preparation time: 30 minutes
Cooking time: 40–50 minutes +
   10–15 minutes standing

500 g (1 lb 2 oz) skinless, boneless
   chicken breasts
1 chicken stock cube, crumbled
40 g (1½ oz) cornflour
450 ml (16 fl oz) skimmed milk
1 bay leaf
8 x 20 g (¾ oz) sheets dried lasagne
40 g (1½ oz) Parmesan cheese,
   freshly grated

For the ratatouille
calorie controlled cooking spray
2 red onions, chopped roughly
1 aubergine, cubed
3 mixed peppers, de-seeded and
   chopped roughly
2 courgettes, chopped roughly
3 garlic cloves, crushed
2 x 400 g cans chopped tomatoes
1 teaspoon dried mixed herbs
salt and freshly ground black pepper

1 Place the chicken breasts in a saucepan, cover with boiling water and add the chicken stock cube. Bring to the boil, cover the pan and remove it from the heat. Leave to stand for 15 minutes. Remove the cooked chicken from the hot stock and leave to cool before slicing.

2 To make the ratatouille, spray a large lidded saucepan with the cooking spray and cook the onions and aubergine for 4 minutes, covered, stirring occasionally.

3 Add the peppers, courgettes and garlic and cook for a further 4 minutes, stirring.

4 Mix in the tomatoes, mixed herbs and seasoning, and simmer for 10 minutes, partially covered.

5 To make a white sauce, place the cornflour in a non-stick saucepan. Gradually blend in the milk, stirring until the mixture is smooth. Add the bay leaf and bring the sauce to the boil, stirring until the sauce has thickened, to avoid lumps forming.

6 Preheat the oven to Gas Mark 4/180°C/fan oven 160°C.

7 To assemble the lasagne, spoon half of the ratatouille into an ovenproof dish measuring around 23 x 30 cm (9 x 12 inches). Top with 4 sheets of lasagne and layer with the rest of the ratatouille, the sliced chicken and 4 more sheets of lasagne. Pour the white sauce over the top and sprinkle with the Parmesan cheese.

8 Bake the lasagne in the oven for 40–50 minutes, until the top is a rich golden brown and the lasagne sheets feel tender when pierced with a skewer or sharp knife.

9 Let the cooked lasagne stand for 10–15 minutes before serving, to make portioning up easier.

CLASSIC POULE
au Pot

Based on a traditional French recipe, a whole chicken is poached in stock with a selection of vegetables to give lovely moist meat, tender veg and a well-flavoured sauce to bring it all together.

 ProPoints values per serving
ProPoints values per recipe 64

Serves 4 with leftovers
Preparation time: 15 minutes
Cooking time: 1 hour 50 minutes

1.4 kg (3 lb) whole chicken
1 **onion**, halved
a few whole black peppercorns
2 bay leaves
700 ml (1¼ pints) chicken stock, made from stock cubes or powder
400 g (14 oz) new **potatoes**, halved
250 g (9 oz) Chantenay **carrots**, trimmed and halved
3 **leeks**, trimmed and cut into large chunks
150 g (5½ oz) frozen **peas**
20 g (¾ oz) cornflour
60 g (2 oz) Weight Watchers reduced fat thick cream
salt and freshly ground black pepper

1 Start by removing the skin from the chicken: follow the method on page 80. Trim off any excess fat and tie the legs together.

2 Place the skinned chicken in a large lidded casserole, breast side down, with the onion, peppercorns, bay leaves, stock and seasoning. Cover, bring to the boil, then reduce the heat and cook at a gentle simmer for 30 minutes. Turn the chicken over carefully and cook for a further 20 minutes.

3 Lift the chicken out of the casserole. Remove and discard the onion, bay leaves and peppercorns, lifting them out with a draining spoon. Add the potatoes, carrots and leeks to the casserole, pushing them down into the liquid. Return the chicken to the casserole, sitting it on top of the vegetables. Cook for 25 minutes or until the vegetables are tender.

4 Lift the chicken and vegetables out on to a serving dish, cover with foil and keep warm.

5 Return the casserole to the heat and boil the liquid for 10 minutes or until it has reduced by about a third. Add the peas to the liquid and bring back to the boil.

6 Meanwhile, blend the cornflour with 1 tablespoon of cold water in a small bowl. Add a little of the hot cooking liquid to the bowl and then pour the cornflour mixture into the casserole. Bring to the boil, stirring, until thickened. Stir in the cream to finish the sauce.

7 Carve the chicken, serving 125 g (4½ oz) meat per person. Serve with the vegetables, and the peas and sauce spooned over.

INDEX